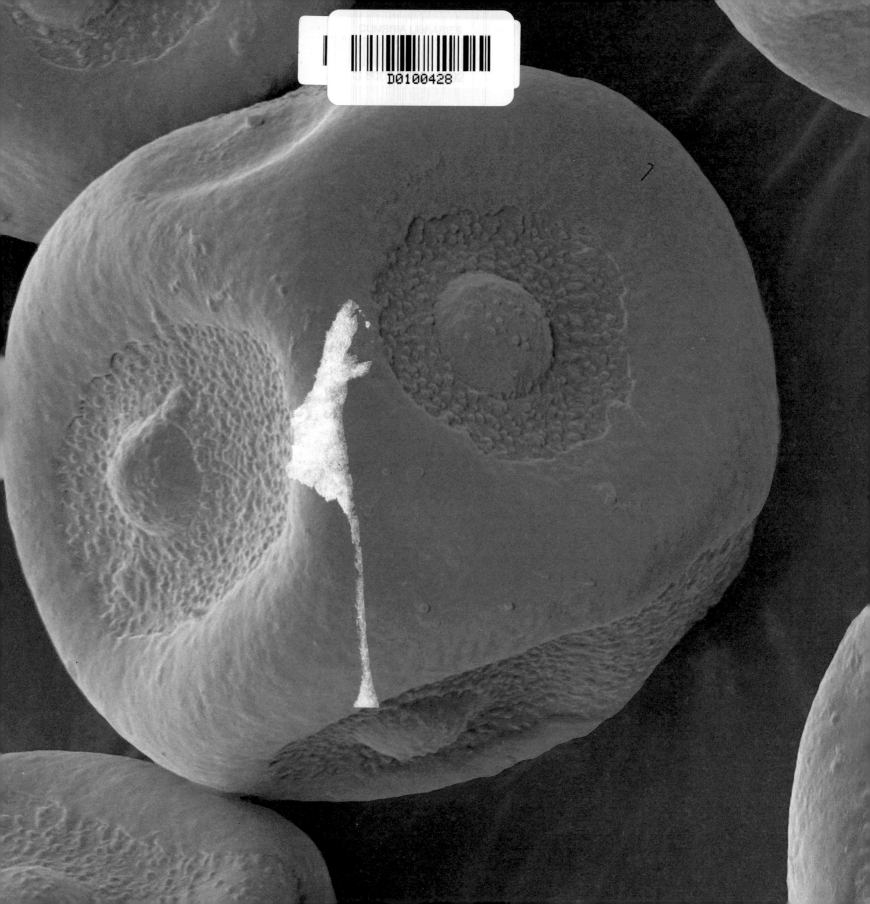

Franklin Watts
First published in Great Britain in 2016 by The Watts Publishing Group

Credits
Series editor: Paul Humphrey
Series designer: sprout.uk.com
Planning and production by Discovery Books Limited
Design and illustration: sprout.uk.com

Photo credits: Ami Images/Science Photo Library: 26–27; Bigstock: 5, 6, 8, 10, 13, 14, 17, 19 (right), 21, 23, 25, 26, 27, 28; Blickwinkel/Alamy Stock Photo: 8–9; CDC/NIAID: 28–29; Clouds Hill Imaging Ltd/Science Photo Library/Getty Images: 6–7; Dartmouth College: 19 (left); Steve Gschmeissner/Science Photo Library: 12–13, 22–23, 24–25; Steve Gschmeissner/Science Photo Library/Alamy Stock Photo: 4–5, 18–19; Sebastian Kaulitzki/Science Photo Library/Alamy Stock Photo: front cover; Lawrence Berkeley National Laboratory: 4; MedicalRF.com/Alamy Stock Photo: 16–17; Marek Mis/Science Photo Library: 20–21; Power & Syred/Science Photo Library: title page, 10–11; NOAA: 22; Sarefo/Creative Commons: 9.

Every attempt has been made to clear copyright. Should there be any inadvertent omission please apply to the publisher for rectification.

ISBN 978 1 4451 5115 1

Printed in China

Franklin Watts
An imprint of
Hachette Children's Group
Part of The Watts Publishing Group
Carmelite House
50 Victoria Embankment
London EC4Y 0DZ

An Hachette UK Company
www.hachette.co.uk

www.franklinwatts.co.uk

Note to the reader: many SEM images use false colours to make the subject more visible. Whenever possible the magnification of images has been added.

Contents

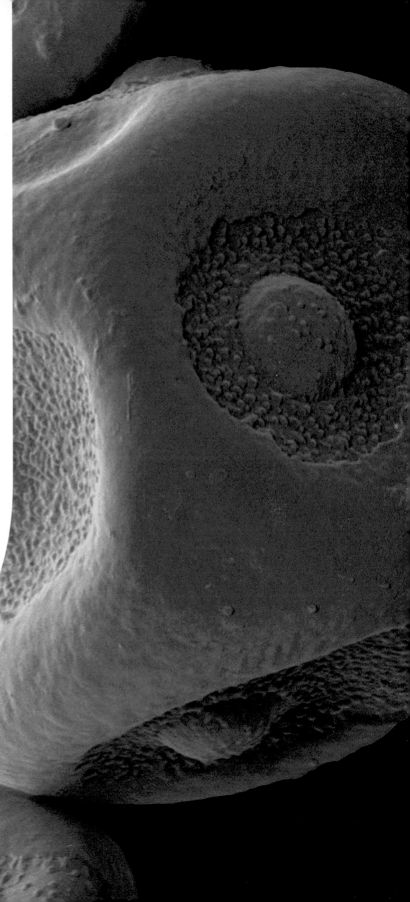

Words in **bold** can be found in
the glossary on page 30.

The world of micro monsters

Home sweet home. It's safe, cosy, familiar ... and full of monsters. You may think you know who lives in your home, but think again. You're about to discover the world of micro monsters that also call your bed, your bathroom and your kitchen 'home'!

Tiny living things you can see only under a microscope are called **microorganisms**. Some of them are micro-animals: insects and other creatures too small to see without a microscope. Other **organisms** are **microbes**: **fungi** and **bacteria** so tiny that you need super-strong microscopes to see them.

Scanning electron microscopes (SEMs) **magnify** things many thousands of times. They can show us some of the micro monsters that live around our homes.

This microscope, the TEAM 0.5 in California, USA, is one of the most powerful microscopes in the world. It can show the inside of an **atom** magnified millions of times.

Monstrous data

Name	Cat flea
Latin name	*Ctenocephalides f...*
Adult length	1–3 mm
Habitat	On and near cats o... other furry animal...
Lifespan	4–10 weeks

Fiendish fleas

Our first monster is sitting pretty right now – on your cat. Nestled into your furry friend is a bloodsucking fiend straight out of a monster movie. Cat fleas latch on tight to cats with comb-like hooks. They pierce cats' skin with their mandibles (jaws) and suck out blood.

Cat fleas have no wings, so when a flea needs to flee, it jumps. Fleas can jump up to 100 times their height. Imagine if you could do that! You'd be able to jump over the London Eye.

Gross or what?

Once a female flea gets a nice meal of fresh blood, she can lay her eggs in the cat's fur. The eggs drop off as the cat moves around, and they hatch in warm dark spots around the home.

5

Dirty dusters

If you look under your bed, you might find a ball of dust or two (or ten). Before you sweep them up, think about this: on every square metre of carpet, there could more than 100,000 dust mites.

But dust mites don't just live UNDER your bed. They like it even better IN your bed, where it's warm and damp. There are probably millions of them in your mattress and on your favourite soft chair right now.

Dust mites are **arachnids** – like spiders and mites, they have eight legs and no wings. They can't drink water, so they need moist air to survive. For food, they like the delicious bits of dead skin that you, your family and your pets shed around your home.

Your pillow may be home to hundreds of thousands of dust mites – enough to make up about 10 per cent of its weight.

Gross or what?

Dust mites turn your skin flakes into liquid to make a monstrous meal of them. They squirt it with **digestive juices** before slurping it up.

Monstrous data

Name	Dust mite
Latin name	*Dermatophagoides*
Adult length	0.2–0.3 mm
Habitat	Carpets, furniture, bedding
Lifespan	10 days (male) to 10 weeks (female)

Dust mites on a carpet, magnified 486 times

Monstrous habitat

Dust mites live in your sofa, your carpets and your bed. They like soft fabrics that trap dust, and their favourite spot is your pillow.

People shed up to .08 grams of skin cells every hour. That's almost 2 grams a day and up to 700 grams a year!

Dusty droppings

Household dust is full of flakes of skin. Eeewww! It also holds lots of dead mites and their poo. Double eeewww! Dust mites get rid of their droppings about twenty times a day. Some people are **allergic** to the droppings.

Claws!

Pseudo means false, so this pseudoscorpion is a false scorpion. It looks like a scorpion because of its fearsome pincers. But those pincers are so small in reality that you'd never see them without a microscope. Pseudoscorpions are arachnids, a group that includes real scorpions, too.

Pseudoscorpions lurk in hidden spots around the home. You might not want to meet one on a dark night, but they are actually quite useful. They are ferocious **predators**, and they eat everything from lice to the **larvae** of pests you might be happy to get rid of.

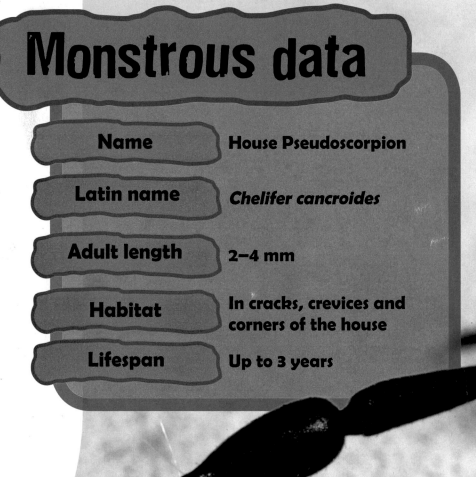

Monstrous data

Name	House Pseudoscorpion
Latin name	*Chelifer cancroides*
Adult length	2–4 mm
Habitat	In cracks, crevices and corners of the house
Lifespan	Up to 3 years

Pincers

Monstrous habitat

In houses, in the bark of trees and other damp, dark places.

8

Pseudoscorpions can have four eyes, two eyes or no eyes at all.

Like spiders, pseudoscorpions spin silk to make cocoons. When it gets cold, they can curl up in a cocoon and wait until it gets warm again before coming out.

Hitchhiker

Pseudoscorpions have a habit of hitchhiking on bigger bugs. Creatures that do this are called phoretic. Not all pseudoscorpions are phoretic, but many do grab a leg and fly around on flies, beetles and other winged creatures. They might even find mites to gobble up as they ride.

Pseudoscorpion

Fly

Monster mites

What's causing that itch? If your pet pup can't stop scratching, you can bet this mitey monster has taken up residence in his ear. Dog ear mites are some of the tiniest arachnids around, but hundreds of them scampering around inside a furry head can make any canine crazy!

Dog ear mites are **parasites**, creatures that live on other living things and feed off them. They are found more in puppies than in adult dogs. And in spite of their name, these monster mites are actually more common in your cat's ear. They can even infect hamsters, rabbits and gerbils.

Monstrous data

Name	Dog ear mite
Latin name	*Otodectes cynotis*
Adult length	0.25 mm
Habitat	Ears of furry mammals
Lifespan	3–4 weeks

One sign that your pet has ear mites is if it shakes its head a lot. Another is sore patches behind the ear, from all the scratching.

Monstrous habitat

Dog ear mites live in and around the ears and sometimes on the skin of dogs, cats and other furry mammals.

Male or female?

A dog ear mite doesn't know if it's male or female until after it **mates**. After a mite hatches from its egg, it becomes first a larva, then a **nymph**. The nymph will find an adult male mite to mate with. Only after mating does it become an adult male or female itself. If it's female, it lays eggs of its own. If it's male, it just trots off around the ear, looking for new nymphs to mate with.

An SEM image of a dog ear mite, magnified 836 times

Gross or what?

Dog ear mites eat doggy ear wax for dinner. UGH!

Pets get mites by hanging out with other pets. The mini-pests just crawl from one animal to the next.

Book munchers

A charming-looking housemate like this one may be close by while you are doing your homework. This booklouse and its fellow students lurk in quiet corners, and they especially like bookshelves full of musty old volumes.

What you're seeing here is the booklouse's head, with its bulging forehead, feelers, and **ocelli**, or simple eyes. Although it looks like an alien from your worst nightmare, the booklouse is fairly harmless as micro monsters go. They live unnoticed in many homes and only become a pest when they start showing up in large numbers.

Monstrous data

Name	**Booklouse**
Latin name	*Psocoptera*
Adult length	**1–2 mm**
Habitat	**Places where mould grows**
Lifespan	**Up to a few months**

A louse is a type of insect with no wings. Some types of lice attach themselves to people or animals and feed on their blood.

Monstrous habitat

Booklice live indoors in hidden corners and bookshelves, and they are often found in old books.

The head of this booklouse is magnified 767 times.

ocelli

The outdoor version of a *booklouse* is a *barklouse*. Barklice live under the bark of trees or in old birds' nests.

Mouldy old books
Booklice eat fungi, and mould is a type of fungi they like a whole lot. When they are lunching in your library, they are actually eating the mould and other fungi that grow on old books.

13

Rotters!

Dry rot is a fearsome fungus that feeds on your home. It causes the wood to crumble, filling it with holes until it looks like an old sponge. Not what you want holding up your walls! People often don't know the rot has set in until it's too late.

Dry rot is a stealthy destroyer. Like many kinds of fungi, it spreads in creeping threads called **hyphae**, the spidery web you can see here. These microscopic threads can spread out for huge distances. As the fungus spreads, it feeds on wood fibres, leaving holes behind.

Gross or what?

In perfect conditions (damp and cool) dry rot can spread as fast as 80 mm a day. Imagine that growing in your floor!

Dry rot can get through plaster or brick walls to infect timbers on the other side.

Monstrous data

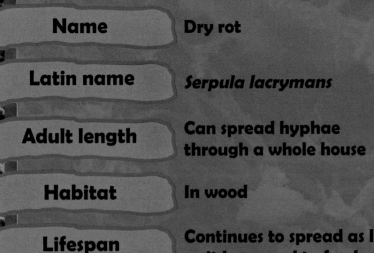

Name	Dry rot
Latin name	*Serpula lacrymans*
Adult length	Can spread hyphae through a whole house
Habitat	In wood
Lifespan	Continues to spread as long as it has wood to feed on

Spore spreader

This reckless rotter produces fruiting bodies, which are pods full of **spores**. Fungi use spores to **reproduce**, or make new fungi, and these pods can pump billions of spores into the air. The spores land around the home, speckling surfaces with reddish powder and finding new places to grow and spread.

Dry rot prefers temperatures of 19 to 22 °C, but it can survive any temperature from 3 to 26 °C.

Monstrous habitat

Dry rot lives in and feeds off beams, floorboards and other wooden parts of buildings. Sometimes it spreads from buildings to old wood in the wild.

Mucky mould

What about finding this monstrous mushroom creeping along the side of your bath? It could well be there right now. Black mould is a fungus that likes to lurk in damp places. Like other moulds, it forms threads called hyphae and gets busy growing and spreading spores.

This mouldy monster just loves your home. It spreads its fungal feelers over wood and plaster, cardboard and wallpaper, tiles and files. Anywhere that water leaks, spills, collects or drips, black mould can appear. This is one super-happy fungus after a flood!

A favourite fodder for black mould outside is hay. Unfortunately horses like h too, and they can get sick f the mould, just like human

Monstrous data

Name	Black mould
Latin name	*Stachybotrys Chartarum*
Adult length	Can spread through a whole building
Habitat	Damp and flooded buildings
Lifespan	As long as there is moisture and a food source

Gross or wh

As if it's not gross enough, black m produces its spores in a slimy head mould is slimy to the touch. The sl sludge is in fact full of spores.

Black mould is not the only mould in your home. There are lots of other types, even in your bed! The most common is *Aspergillus fumigatus*. Like black mould, *Aspergillus* makes some people very ill.

Fungus fever

People living in homes where black mould lurks often get quite ill. They might think they have colds, flu or allergies. In fact it's mould making them feel mouldy. Some people get fevers or stomach upsets, others get rashes or aches and pains and still others wheeze and cough.

Monstrous habitat

Black mould lives in buildings that have leaks, damp air or flood damage.

Pretty pollen

Where would you see a funny face like this one in your home? The answer is all around you, right now, but they are too tiny to see. Trillions of microscopic grains of pollen fill the air in spring and at other times of year, too.

Pollen grains come from plants. The grains contain some of the cells that plants need to reproduce. When pollen from one plant reaches another plant of the same **species**, it joins with that plant's cells to produce new plants. Pollen has two main ways of getting about. Heavier, sticky pollen attaches to insects when they visit a flower for nectar, and it gets carried to another plant. Lighter kinds of pollen just blow through the air to find another plant.

The smallest pollen grain comes from a forget-me-not flower. It is only about .006 mm across.

Monstrous data

Name	Pollen of flowering currant
Latin name	*Ribes sanguineum* pollen
Adult length	0.04 mm
Habitat	In plants
Lifespan	One season

Monstrous habitat

Plants everywhere produce pollen and it gets scattered all over the place, including in your home.

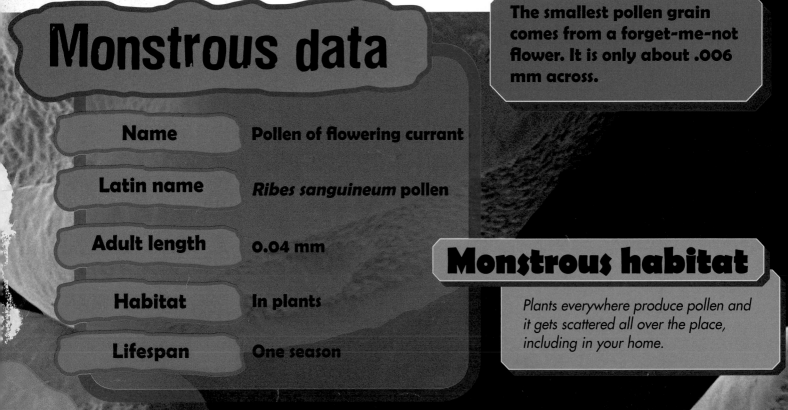

Allergies in the air

Do you get bothered by **allergies** in the spring? You are probably having a reaction to all the pollen in the air. Many pollens are so small that they are easy to inhale. They cause people's noses to get bunged up, and their eyes get red and sore. Pollens from grasses cause hay fever, a very common allergy.

Pollen is in all household dust. Some people with dust allergies are actually allergic to the pollen that blows in from outside.

Water wheels

When you run water from the tap, imagine all the microorganisms that may be in just one drop. This whirling wonder, known as a rotifer, sometimes slips through water filters into household water along with bacteria and other microbes. They might be swimming in your rain gutter, too.

Rotifers, also known as wheel animals, are among the smallest animals in the world. All rotifers have what look like rotating wheels on their heads. In fact the whizzing wig is a crown of fast-moving hairs called cilia, which are used to sense and catch prey. If a rotifer senses a tasty titbit nearby, it waves its cilia like mad. This draws the water and the prey into the rotifer's waiting jaws.

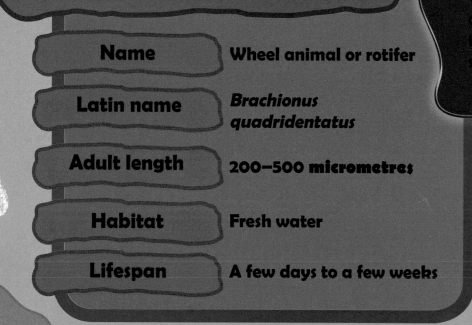

Monstrous data

Name	Wheel animal or rotifer
Latin name	*Brachionus quadridentatus*
Adult length	200–500 **micrometres**
Habitat	Fresh water
Lifespan	A few days to a few weeks

Gross or what?

When you look at a rotifer, you get a good look at its insides because it's transparent. You can even see all the stuff in its stomach!

All rotifers have a foot, which some species use to anchor themselves to surfaces and wait for passing prey.

During dry periods, rotifers become **dormant**. Once they are dormant, they can stay inactive for many years.

Rotifers live mostly in fresh water or in wet soil. A few live in salt water.

Stomach

Foot

This rotifer has been magnified 912 times.

Cilia

Copycats

Among rotifers there aren't many males. The females can reproduce with or without help from males. Females simply make eggs, a few at a time. Within a day, the eggs hatch and out pop new rotifers, identical to their mother.

21

Horned horrors

This micro monster looks spiky and spooky, but it's only one cell high. That's pretty small! Diatoms are everywhere in water. A type of **algae**, they are more like plants than animals, and they make their own food by **photosynthesis**. As a result of photosynthesis, they produce a lot of the oxygen in our air.

Even though they have only one cell, these microbes form some pretty dazzling displays. Under a microscope, a group of diatoms can look like a jewel collection. This is because the outer wall of their cell is a shell, called a frustule, made from a hard **mineral** that forms shiny shapes. If a diatom dies or discards its shell, the empty frustule is left behind.

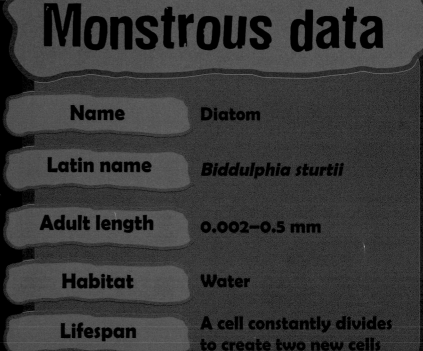

Monstrous habitat

Diatoms exist anywhere that there is water and light. These ones are living among crystals of ice.

Monstrous data

Name	Diatom
Latin name	*Biddulphia sturtii*
Adult length	0.002–0.5 mm
Habitat	Water
Lifespan	A cell constantly divides to create two new cells

Scientists think there are about 100,000 species of diatoms. They are a source of food for many other microorganisms.

When a diatom divides to reproduce, one of the new diatoms is smaller than the other because one half of the frustule is always slightly smaller.

Dental diatoms

People collect fossilised diatom frustules from the sea to use in many ways. From cat litter to cough syrup and polish to plastic, ground-up diatoms are everywhere in your home. Diatom frustules can soundproof your walls and filter water. And because it's good at cleaning things, diatom powder is even used in soap and toothpaste!

Kitchen killers

You'll find these in the kitchen, but they're not a pile of sausages! These are **E.coli**, a type of bacteria that lives everywhere: in you, in your food and all over your home. They're so tiny you'd need a strong microscope to see them.

Bacteria have only one plan in life: to reproduce. They reproduce so fast and in such large numbers it makes your mind boggle. Let's just say your kitchen is a bacteria breeding ground, and billions of them are busy tucking into your food and multiplying as quickly as they can. They grow extra fast on warm food, so don't leave your dinner out!

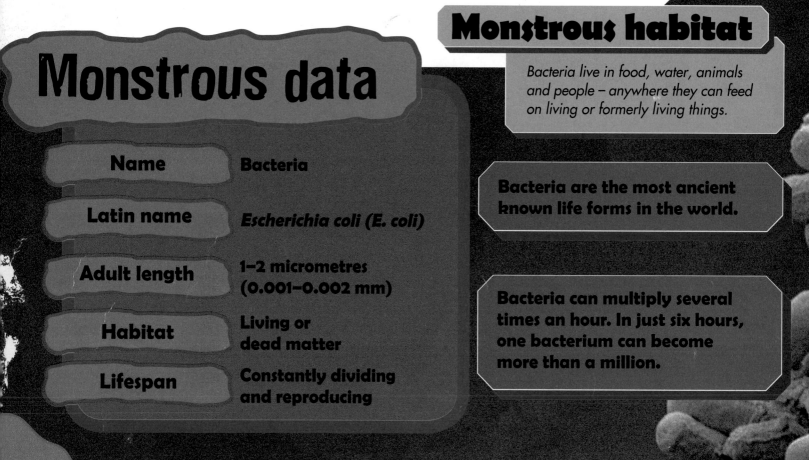

Monstrous data

Name	Bacteria
Latin name	*Escherichia coli (E. coli)*
Adult length	1–2 micrometres (0.001–0.002 mm)
Habitat	Living or dead matter
Lifespan	Constantly dividing and reproducing

Monstrous habitat

Bacteria live in food, water, animals and people – anywhere they can feed on living or formerly living things.

Bacteria are the most ancient known life forms in the world.

Bacteria can multiply several times an hour. In just six hours, one bacterium can become more than a million.

Gross or what?

Don't look too closely at your kitchen sponge. One study found a kitchen sponge holds thousands of bacteria in every spongy square centimetre. Give it a wash in hot water, or even better, put it in the microwave for two minutes.

Tummy terrors

Most bacteria are harmless and even good for us. The natural world wouldn't work without bacteria to process stuff. Some bacteria clean water. Others, such as *Lactobacillus acidophilus*, help your body to fight infection. But some, like *E. coli*, can make you very ill. If they get from your kitchen into you, they can cause a horrible upset stomach or infection.

An SEM image of *E. coli* bacteria that have been magnified 9,765 times

Virus attack!

If it's hard to imagine thousands of bacteria on a speck of sponge, then imagine this: a monster so micro that it makes **BACTERIA** look big! That's what **viruses** are. The green viruses in this picture (right) are attacking a bacterium cell.

Of course, in some cases that's a good thing. Viruses that attack bacteria are called bacteriophages. The bacteriophages you see here can kill off **host** bacteria so they won't make a person ill. But other viruses actually cause illnesses, such as colds and chicken pox.

Monstrous data

Name	Bacteriophage virus
Latin name	*Bacillus phage*
Adult length	30–250 **nanometres** (0.00003–0.00025 mm)
Habitat	In living cells
Lifespan	Can only survive as long as host cell is alive

Bacteriophages look a bit like lunar-landing vehicles. They have spiky 'legs' for poking into their host and a multi-sided capsule on top.

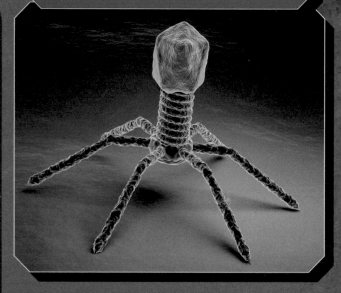

The Spanish Flu was a virus that killed 20–50 million people in one year. Starting in 1918, it spread rapidly around the world.

Secret code

Viruses cannot survive without a living cell, but once they find their cell, they destroy it. First, the virus attaches itself to its host. Then it injects the host with its own special code. This instructs the unsuspecting host cell to reproduce the virus. The virus fills up the host until it bursts open and dies, and out pops the virus to infect other cells!

Monstrous habitat

Bacteriophages need to get inside bacteria to reproduce. They are found anywhere in your home where there are lots of bacteria hosts, such as on food in the kitchen.

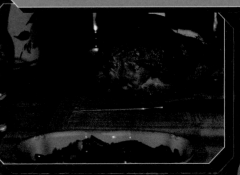

Gross or what?

Viruses can spread when people sneeze or cough without covering their mouth and spray you with their germs. You can also pick up a virus by touching an infected surface.

Bathroom baddies

Here's a micro monster that will make you want to have a good wash! These colourful spheres are in fact bacteria called staphylococci, or staph for short. Some types of staph are harmless, but others cause nasty skin infections and even serious illnesses, such as meningitis.

Many people carry staph around on their skin. It can be passed between people, especially in bathrooms. Make sure you wash your hands really well, with hot water and soap, after going to the toilet, so you don't pick up or spread staph and other germs.

Gross or what?

There are up to a million bacteria per square centimetre on some areas of the toilet. YUCK!

Bacteria come in three basic shapes: rod, spiral or sphere (ball-shaped). Bacteria spheres are called *cocci*, which comes from a Greek word for berries.

Monstrous data

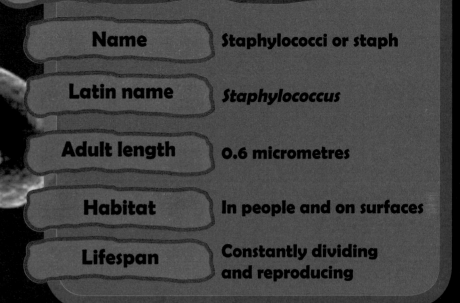

Name	Staphylococci or staph
Latin name	*Staphylococcus*
Adult length	0.6 micrometres
Habitat	In people and on surfaces
Lifespan	Constantly dividing and reproducing

Monstrous habitat

Staph lives on unclean surfaces and on living organisms.

Many kinds of bacteria can lie dormant for years without any problems. If they don't have the right conditions to feed and reproduce, they just shut down until things improve.

Beating bacteria

Doctors began to beat bad bacteria after the discovery of penicillin in 1928. The scientist Alexander Fleming (1881–1955) found that some mould called *Penicillium notatum* growing on staph was killing it. He had discovered antibiotics, which we use today to fight bacterial infections.

Glossary

algae organisms, including seaweeds, that are similar to plants

allergic to have an allergy

allergy a reaction to eating, touching or breathing something that only some people get, for example a reaction to peanuts, cats or pollen

arachnid group of small animals, including spiders, scorpions and mites, with eight legs and two parts to their bodies

atom the smallest particle of any matter

bacteria one-celled organisms, such as *E. coli*, that are the most numerous living things in the world

cell the tiny unit that living things are made of

digestive juices liquids produced by the digestive system to break down food into nutrients an animal can absorb

dormant the inactive state of living things when they are not moving, feeding or reproducing

fungus (pl: fungi) an organism, such as mould, that lives on and feeds off living or dead plants and animals and reproduces with spores

habitat the place or type of place where an organism usually lives

host an organism that is home to a parasite or a cell that is home to a virus

hyphae threads some fungi use to spread on their host

larva stage of an insect between egg and adult

magnify to make something look bigger

mate join together to reproduce

microbe any microscopic living thing that is not an animal

micrometre the measurement of length that is one-thousandth of a millimetre and sometimes called a micron

microorganism a living thing too small to see without a microscope

microscopic too small to see without a microscope

mineral a solid non-living substance, such as salt

mite tiny arachnids that often live on bigger animals

nanometre the measurement of length that is one-millionth of a millimetre

nymph an immature insect

ocelli an insect's simple eyes that sense light and movement

organism any living or formerly living thing

paralyse make something unable to move

parasite a living thing that lives on or in another living thing and uses its host as food

photosynthesis the process by which plants use light to make food from water and carbon dioxide

predator an animal or microbe that hunts or catches another living thing for food

prey an animal or microbe hunted and caught by another living thing for food

reproduce to make new living things, such as when two people produce a baby, or plants produce seeds that grow into new plants

rotifer a micro-animal identified by the wheels of cilia on its head

species group of animals or plants with the same qualities that can reproduce together, such as humans or bulldogs or tulips

spores seeds of fungi and some other living things

virus microbe that multiplies by infecting the cells of organisms

Further information

Books

Complete Book of the Microscope
by Kirsteen Rogers (Usborne, 2012)

Horrible Science: Microscopic Monsters
by Nick Arnold (Scholastic 2014)

In the Home (Under the Microscope)
by Sabrina Crewe (Chelsea Clubhouse, 2010)

Websites

http://www.childrensuniversity.manchester.ac.uk/
interactives/science/microorganisms/
Learn all about microorganisms at the Children's University of Manchester.

http://commtechlab.msu.edu/sites/dlc-me/zoo/index.html
Visit the Microbe Zoo!

http://education.denniskunkel.com/catalog/
Lots of great photos from one of the world's best micro-photographers.

http://www.microscopy-uk.org.uk/micropolitan/index.html
Wander around the Micropolitan Museum and find 'the smallest page on the web'.

Every effort has been made by the publisher to ensure that these websites contain no inappropriate or offensive material. However, because of the nature of the Internet, it is impossible to guarantee that the content of these sites will not be altered. We strongly advise that Internet access is supervised by a responsible adult.

Measuring the microscopic world

It's hard to imagine how small micrometres and nanometres really are. This picture helps you to see how they compare to a millimetre. Millimetres are pretty tiny themselves, but they are GIANT compared to nanometres. In every millimetre, there are one million nanometres!

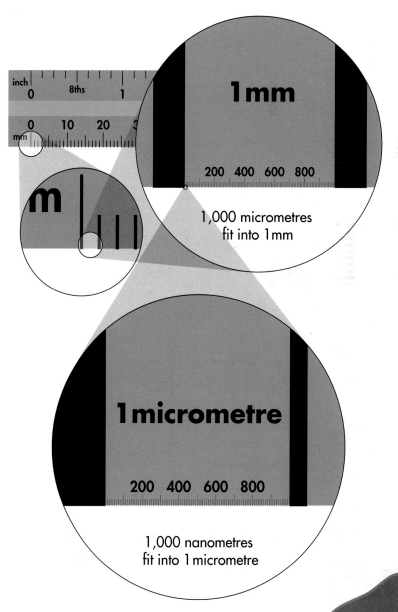

1,000 micrometres fit into 1mm

1,000 nanometres fit into 1 micrometre

Index

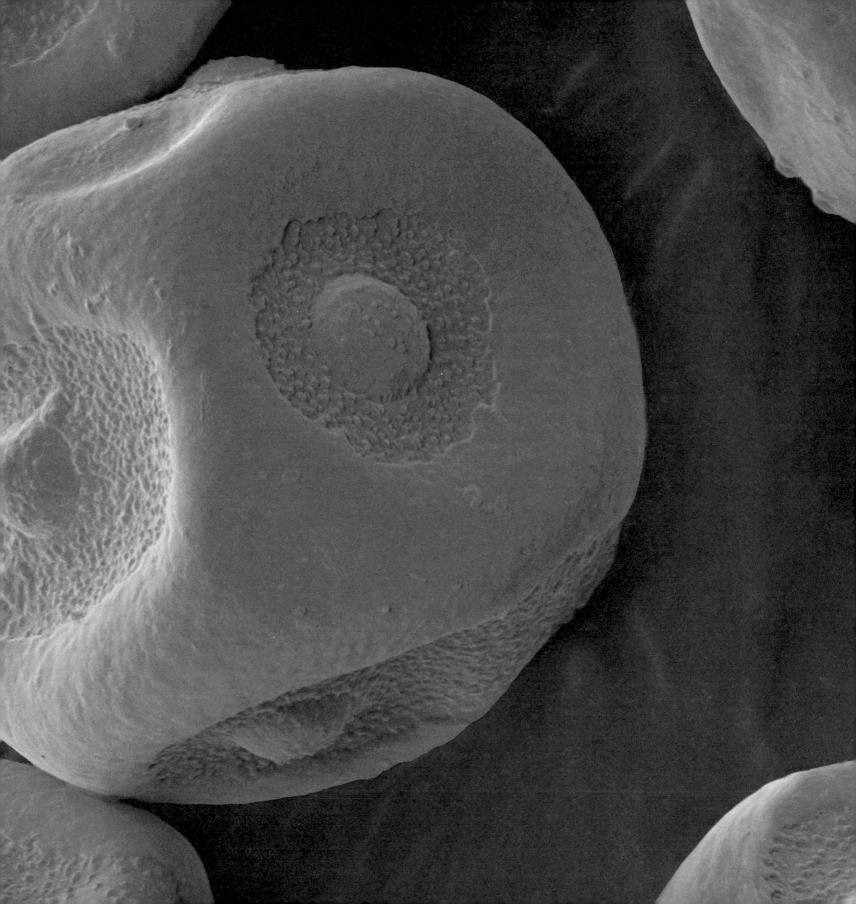